TIME ROBBERS

TIME ROBBERS

JOHN KNAUF, JR

PALMETTO
PUBLISHING
Charleston, SC
www.PalmettoPublishing.com

© 2024 John Knauf, Jr.
All rights reserved.
No portion of this book may be reproduced,
stored in a retrieval system, or transmitted in
any form by any means–electronic, mechanical,
photocopy, recording, or other–except for
brief quotations in printed reviews,
without prior permission of the author.

Paperback ISBN: 979-8-8229-3174-9

TIME ROBBERS
Defining and preventing potential time wasters

DREAM CHASERS
INSPIRING QUOTATIONS
AND
HUMOR ATTEMPTS

Time: Protect it or loose it. All any of us have is our time.

Who manages our time?

This training can provide techniques to manage our time. We can refer to this manual to respond to potential time robbers including ourselves.

No one graduates from this training…….
this is an equipping for life. Virgil Geogics says
"Time speeds away irrevocably"

CONTENTS

Forward ix
Overview of Time Robbers 1
My Journey by John Knauf, Jr. 3
My Journey by Les Connell 5
My Journey by Darrell Badger 9
Chapter 1 - Dreamers 11
Chapter 2 - Just Stubborn 12
Chapter 3 - Opinions 13
Chapter 4 - Definition Of Emergencies 14
Chapter 5 - If We're Smart 15
Chapter 6 - Don't Assume 16
Chapter 7 - What is Working Smart/Hard? 17
Chapter 8 - Schedule vs. Agenda? 18
Chapter 9 - Training on Pausing 19
Chapter 10 - What is a Muse? 20
Chapter 11 - What is an Introvert?
                 What is an Extrovert? 21
Chapter 12 - Envy vs. Contentment 22
Chapter 13 - What is a Leader? 23
Chapter 14 - Healthy Delegation vs.
                 Ruthless Delegation 24

Chapter 15 - Pausing for Compassion or Empathy............ 25

Chapter 16 - The Value of Persistence................................ 26

Chapter 17 - How to Move From Victim to Victory 27

Chapter 18 - Money vs. The Love of Money 28

Chapter 19 - Are We Really Listening? 29

Chapter 20 - What is Procrastination? 30

Chapter 21 - Unrealistic Expectations of People Can Be
Pre-Existing Disappointments 31

Chapter 22 - How to Respond Kindly to Interruptions
and Those Who Would Rob Your Time........ 32

Inspiring Quotations 33

Time Wasted 35

"Religion Compared to Relationship" 37

Do It Anyway 39

Humor Attemps 40

A Few Key Passages From The Holy Scriptures................. 41

FORWARD

This manual is a compilation of random thoughts from a dream I had regarding time robbers. This is a reference manual for you to read and re-visit whenever you want.

We initially thought the dream would have a secular interpretation, but as we got more involved in this project, we realized it was from the Lord, our God.

This manual helps you with the mystery history of the dream zone. Many who have experienced the dream zone have pencil and paper at hand at night to record messages. Many inventions and books have their inspiration from dreams.

ACTS 2:17…..In the last days God says I will pour out my spirit on your sons and daughters. I will proclaim my message. Your young men will see visions, and your old men will have dreams (Joel 2:28). Then after doing these things, I will pour out my spirit on all people. God is not a man that he should lie.

– John Knauf, Jr.

OVERVIEW OF TIME ROBBERS

When people look at this manual, the goal is for them to get a strong impression that this manual is not just a "want" but a "need" in their lives. We all need training in this area because <u>all we have is our time</u>!

This training will enable you to screen people's interferences and demands on your time, by turning their efforts to control you into ways you can maintain control of YOUR OWN TIME, thereby producing positive experiences from a vast encounter of people's efforts to rob your time. Sometimes we experience people who may be offended by our methods. However, we contend that being offended is a personal choice! We have to protect our time because time is a precious commodity.

This training provides honest ways of moving on from unnecessary dialogue. We want to pursue the goal of NOT "wasting precious time."

Interruptions aren't always negative! We surely can learn from the people around us who are potential time robbers.

Following are the journeys of the three contributors to this manual.

MY JOURNEY

By

John Knauf, Jr.

I grew up with two brothers and two sisters. I won't speak for my siblings but the enemy of my soul (Satan) started grooming me at a young age. I went down and down eventually becoming a lost human in the 60's. In 1973, I surrendered into a relationship with Jesus Christ, and emerged into a "born again" experience. Some have described the post born again experience is like Lazarus coming out of the grave! I fit that description….my spirit is willing by my flesh is still weak.

One of my favorite sections of the Bible is the 23rd Psalm; written by King David, who was a shepherd boy who killed Goliath. It is the substance of this Psalm that carries eternal power. I once was lost but now I'm saved. I did not earn it and I certainly don't deserve it.

When I was young, like many, I was a renegade. I didn't know what to do; I wanted to go into the Navy. They wouldn't take me; the only choice was the Army. My dad, a Navy vet, drove me to the recruiting station in L.A.

I said, "Dad, I'll either go into the Army or go into commercial fishing. He was fine either way. When I got up in line, ready to get my physical, I began to realize that I was inches away from going to Vietnam. So I got out of line and went downstairs and got into Dad's car. I remember him saying nothing when I said I want to go commercial fishing.

After years of fishing on several boats from San Pedro, CA to Astoria, Oregon. When we were on strike as fishermen, I did handyman work for Adeline Sather who introduced me to a relationship with Jesus Christ. She had a home in Salem, OR, where I could stay while I went back to college. I worked at various jobs and assisted her brother George. While in college there, I went from a "C" average to a 3.6 GPA. I can still hear George's voice confronting me when I was not pulling my weight because I was working at the cannery at night, working at a cabinet shop during the day, and had responsibilities at the house. "You're procrastinating" (see chapter 20 on procrastinating).

"Some succeed because they are destined to, but most succeed because they are determined to." (author unknown)

MY JOURNEY

By

Les Connell

On August 8, 2020 the Almeda Wildfire swept through the small communities of Ashland, Talent, Phoenix and Medford, here in SW Oregon, utterly destroying over 2,400 homes and 200 businesses, and taking the lives of 3 individuals.

Our family business, the Northridge Center senior assisted living facility, was the largest business to be destroyed. Northridge Center housed 52 elderly and disabled residents.

It had been an unseasonably hot and dry summer in SW Oregon. Many areas were suffering from an extended drought, and water supplies were diminished throughout the beautiful Rogue Valley. In the wee hours of the morning on August 8, the wind came up with gusts up to 40MPH.

Later that morning, arsonists ignited a fire in Ashland which spread rapidly north towards Medford as it was fueled by the wind.

There were dramatic failures of the governmental emergency management systems. We were never notified to evacuate Northridge Center. It was only thanks to the wisdom of my daughter, Memory Dent, the executive director of Northridge, who placed a call to 911 to see if we might be at risk. After

11-minutes on hold, the 911 operator came on the line, and said to evacuate everyone immediately.

Memory got right on the intercom and instructed all residents and staff to drop everything and immediately head to the parking lot and board our two wheelchair busses. As soon as she hung up, the power went out in the building.

As we were driving to the designated evacuation site, our smart phones began pinging, notifying us that the smoke alarms and sprinkler systems had been activated.

All 52 residents and the staff were safely evacuated.

But that was not the end of the story….it was only the beginning.

Several months before the fire, our insurance agent called advising us that we were under-insured! Of course I knew that they just wanted to raise the premium. But they came down and convinced us that we were indeed under-insured.

So, we increased the coverage, and several months later the entire facility was destroyed in the Almeda fire. The insurance was sufficient to pay off the balance of the mortgage and purchase an older but much larger facility adjacent to the hospital! Enough insurance was left over to continue to provide income for the livelihood for our family and restore this older building to the beautiful and elegant 70-apartment facility it is today.

....

On May 2, 1965, I made the most important decision of my life....I surrendered it to Jesus Christ. Has everything been rosy since then....by NO means....however, everything has been guided by the hand of almighty God. The Holy Scriptures say "All things work together for the good" and we have certainly found that to be true.

The days following the fire were indeed "black" days. Our family business of 40 years was gone, and along with it, our livelihoods.

But an ancient verse of scripture written over 4,000 years ago, kept coming up and sustaining our family: Proverbs 3: 5-6: *"Trust in the Lord with all your heart and lean not on your own understanding; in all your ways acknowledge him and he will make your paths straight."*

....

Talk about an event that steals our time! There is another ancient verse in the Bible that comforted us during the recovery from the fire: Joel 2:25: *"And I will make up for the years that the locust have eaten......"* Our fire was destructive like the swarms of locusts that plagued the nation of Israel in the time of the prophet Joel. That scripture goes on to say *"Return to me now, while there is time. Give me all your hearts."* The people had lived in rebellion until that time, but when they turned back to Him, he restored those lost years. And that's exactly what He did for us after the fire.

Interruptions continue to be a part of our daily lives, and they often come at the worst time possible. And yet, often times I end up being grateful for them because they bring me information that is important.

That is what this manual is all about. Interruptions are hard to avoid. But the important thing is how we respond to them. Read on and I trust you find jewels of wisdom herein that help you deal with daily interruptions and things that rob your time.

– Les Connell
President, Northridge Senior Living

MY JOURNEY

By

Darrell Badger

My journey began shortly before the conclusion of World War II. I was born into a family of an older brother and amazing parents. My young and informative years were spent on cattle ranches. During which time, my parents taught me the values of hard work, wise use of time and most important, of all….to have a Personal Relationship with Jesus.

I have had an interesting and challenging life. I have been a pizza chef, tree surgeon, platoon sergeant in the US Army, a police officer, a cowboy, worker in the Prudhoe Bay Oil Fields, and lastly, manager of petroleum operations for Grange Co-op in the Rogue Valley in SW Oregon. I thank the Lord for seeing me through my years and always walking beside me.

I thank the Lord and my parents for their support, guidance and for teaching me about how to recognize and control the "Time Robbers".

– Darrell Badger

The following pages will help you navigate potential time robbers because all we have is our time…. a precious commodity. The following few chapters will explore definitions of words as they relate to interruptions and time robbers.

CHAPTER 1
DREAMERS

This manual is dedicated to the many dreamers and visionary people who didn't give up, but kept following their dreams.

Most of us spend up to 1/4th of our lives dreaming. Most of our dreams are crazy and we usually can't remember any of them.

I've looked at the dream realm throughout history. Here are just a few examples:

- Many say that Einstein's Theory of Relativity came from a dream.

- In 1845, Elias Hew was directed in a dream to invent the sewing machine.

- Double Helix said he dreamt of the structure of DNA.

- Frecnecyn August Kekule developed the Benzene compound from a dream in 1890.

- Leonard Thompson and other visionaries on his team, were the first to inject insulin into a 14-year-old boy who was dying from the incurable disease diabetes, thus saving countless lives since then.

CHAPTER 2
JUST STUBBORN

Nearly everyone can deal with positive outcomes. Our team were all raised as optimists (the cup is half full instead of half empty). But we do know the challenge of being a pessimist. We don't accept that people are too old to change. I've seen change come where we never thought it was possible. We will never buy the general statement: "they are just stubborn" …. they will never change their ways.

CHAPTER 3
OPINIONS

Everyone has their own opinions. The definition of opinion is "view, belief, conviction, persuasion, sentiment of judgment one holds true". Opinion implies "thought out but still open to dispute". View suggests a subjective opinion.

People who interrupt us and steal our time, are usually certain that their opinion is of more value than ours, and therefore justifies the interruption. A good listener will pause and listen to their opinion before he weighs their thoughts and decides how to respond. This manual has suggestions regarding how to respond…..see Chapter 22.

CHAPTER 4
DEFINITION OF EMERGENCIES

- An unforeseen combination of circumstances or the resulting state that calls for immediate action.

- An urgent need for assistance or relief (example: the mayor declared a state of emergency).

CHAPTER 5
IF WE'RE SMART

If we're smart, we learn from our mistakes. If we're wise, we learn from others' mistakes.

We should improve through time, and learn how to respond instead of reacting to mistakes. When we observe the situation, we redirect and adjust (see Persistence……chapter16). One of the great things in life is that we can learn every day.

CHAPTER 6
DON'T ASSUME

Don't assume life interruptions are always negative.

My entire family has been so into interruptions that at a family reunion, a big sign said "Don't talk while I'm interrupting."

This manual will help all of us navigate through life's interruptions. There is a difference between protecting our time and being unkind.

CHAPTER 7
WHAT IS WORKING SMART/HARD?

It's one thing to accomplish a smart way of handling chores, then being content. It's important to work smart to maintain time, but if you work both smart AND hard, you will have <u>significant</u> progress.

CHAPTER 8
SCHEDULE VS. AGENDA?

A <u>schedule</u> is a written or printed list or inventory timetable which includes times, dates, priority, flight departures, etc.

An <u>agenda</u> is similar to a schedule but involves more planning and not letting things get in the way. A schedule and an agenda may generally be used interchangeably.

This is a reference manual that needs to be revisited periodically as no one can master this subject matter in one sitting.

CHAPTER 9
TRAINING ON PAUSING

<u>Very important!</u> It takes discipline and restraint to think before you speak! Pausing, or musing gives you time to gather your response and avoid being impulsive.

CHAPTER 10
WHAT IS A MUSE?

It is to be absorbed in thought, thinking about something carefully; an imaginary force that gives someone ideas and helps them write, paint, or to make music, etc. Meditating on the things of God is the best source of inspiration for a creative response.

CHAPTER 11
WHAT IS AN INTROVERT? WHAT IS AN EXTROVERT?

<u>Introvert</u>: A typically reserved or quiet person who tends to be meditative and enjoys spending time alone.

<u>Extrovert</u>: being concerned with the social and physical environment; an outgoing, gregarious person who thrives in dynamic environments and seeks to maximize social engagements.

CHAPTER 12
ENVY VS. CONTENTMENT

Envy: A painful or resentful awareness of an advantage enjoyed by another, joined with a desire to possess the same advantage.

Contentment: A state of happiness or satisfaction. Being at ease, at peace, even in the midst of chaos. Ignoring anxiety but not being delusional. The Challenge is to look for the good side of situations.

:

CHAPTER 13
WHAT IS A LEADER?

I once had the privilege of going to hear a great motivational speaker. You may have heard him in person or read one of his books. His name was Zig Ziegler. Here are a couple of his quotes:

"You sometimes need a checkup from the neck up."

"You should get rid of that stinkin' thinkin'"

Simple quotes, but if applied among many other Zig quotes could change your life.

Another sign of a leader is not taking all the credit for success but learning from defeat, and being ready to lay down their lives for their followers.

Leaders keep their heads, and their focus in life's challenges. They recognize there is no way but to go forward. No retreating or feeling like quitting, but quitting, there is a well of supernatural strength the human can tap into whether in victory or in defeat!

A leader is defined by protecting their followers and managing vengeance. A good leader loves the Lord more than himself, and keeps Him in the forefront of every decision or action. God is the ultimate leader.

CHAPTER 14
HEALTHY DELEGATION VS. RUTHLESS DELEGATION

Advantages of Healthy Delegation

Developing other workers into better managers, freeing up their time, improving motivational morale, helping the timely completion of tasks, enhancing decision-making and allowing productivity.

Ruthless delegation results in time robbing.

Using your own power and position to manipulate worker disadvantages results in lackluster performance of a worker, the lack of enough time to train a worker, and the risk of putting the wrong person in charge.

CHAPTER 15
PAUSING FOR COMPASSION OR EMPATHY

Compassion is sympathy to help others in their distress with a desire to alleviate it.

Empathy is putting yourself in what another person is going through.

CHAPTER 16
THE VALUE OF PERSISTENCE

Quote by Calvin Coolidge:
"Nothing in the world can take the place of persistence."

Talent will not. Nothing is more common than unsuccessful men (people) with talent.

Genius will not. Unrewarded genius is almost a proverb.

Education will not. The world is full of educated derelicts.

Persistence and determination alone are omnipotent.

CHAPTER 17
HOW TO MOVE FROM VICTIM TO VICTORY

The only way to consistently be in the mode of victory instead of victim is not to think you have this training down…this is a day by day, night by night process of using this manual with others whether it be support groups, family, friends, etc. if someone tries to steal our time, our goal should be to not allow it. They might become "TIME ROBBERS".

Moving from victim to victor is caring enough for people to help them constructively without judging. Aways remember that the only way to true victory is through the Lord. With His help we can overcome and accomplish anything.

CHAPTER 18
MONEY VS. THE LOVE OF MONEY

Money is a tool. An important piece of advancing visions and goals. You either have it or you need to get it to address the goals you feel you should have in life.

<u>The love of money is selfish</u>…being a taker instead of a giver. The opposite of the love of money is enjoying the reciprocity of giving. Sometimes we just need to learn how to receive. If we don't learn to receive, we are potentially ROBBING the giver of the experience of giving. We need to learn to be good money managers…not hurting people, but helping them whether it be our family, friends, enemies, etc.

A need does not represent a calling on our lives. Just because you see a need, doesn't necessarily mean you need to be the one to fill it. You are not the only one who can fill the needs.

CHAPTER 19
ARE WE REALLY LISTENING?

Am I really listening…..keeping in mind that we can do all things through Christ who strengthens us. This is a lifetime process. We will make plenty of missteps. Remember that good can be the enemy of perfect!

A very common problem in encountering time robbers or potential ones is when we communicate, we think of other things, or just look for opportunities to jump in. Remember to welcome practice, because practicing is your friend. The steps in this manual will enable you to recognize potential time robbers and how to respond to them (see chapter 22).

It's natural to not really be listening, but just waiting for an opening to jump in. I'm better than this person, etc. I could go on. I think you get the drift!

CHAPTER 20
WHAT IS PROCRASTINATION?

Procrastination robs our time because it lacks structure or ability to motivate us to complete usually unpleasant tasks. Procrastination is at times linked to rumination or becoming fixated with negative thoughts. If we address it, its usually not as difficult as we expected.

CHAPTER 21

UNREALISTIC EXPECTATIONS OF PEOPLE CAN BE PRE-EXISTING DISAPPOINTMENTS

This is so common. "Don't count your chickens before the eggs hatch." If we expect too much from people around us, we will be disappointed.

We can give you solid advice: Love people unconditionally as Christ Loved Us. Jesus said "Love your enemies." That sums it up.

CHAPTER 22

How To Respond Kindly To Interruptions And Those Who Would Rob Your Time

Following are some possible responses:

- I apologize, but I've got some other pressing demands right now. Can I get back to you later?

- I'm sorry I'm so busy today, that I don't really have the time right now. Would you forgive me if we talked later?

- You know what? I have a meeting coming up that I'm not ready for. Could you please excuse me?

- Oh My! I've got a project deadline that is looming. Can we get together later in the week?

- I don't want to be rude, but my schedule today is tight. Could I call you tomorrow?

- I'm slammed today. What's your schedule like the next couple of days?

- If an interruption is going on too long and is not fruitful, get up and politely excuse yourself to tend to a priority.

The key is being kind. (see chapter 15). Even if the interruption is about something of which you have no interest, still be kind.

INSPIRING QUOTATIONS

"Tell me what you think about money and I will tell you what you think about God, for these two are closely related. A man's heart is closer to his wallet than anything else. If a person gets his attitude toward money straight, it will straighten out almost every other area in his life."
– Billy Graham

"God loves details! It is in the details that we discern His hand of providence - - ruling, directing, providing, sustaining, preventing surprises. What may look catastrophic from one point of view will appear from another angle to be the outworking of a plan of which God is in full control."
– Derek Thomas

"If sinners are zealous in their sins should not saints be zealous for their God? If the things of time can stir up human passion, should not the realities of eternity have a greater and more tremendously moving force for us?"
– Charles Spurgeon

"There are a good many ways which would not be worth bothering about if I were going to live only seventy years, but which I better bother about very seriously if I'm gonna live forever."
– C.S.Lewis

"When it comes to my salvation, all I need is Jesus plus the church. When people preach all you need is Jesus, they cut you and I off from one of the greatest sources of healing which is the Body of Christ. Don't go it alone…..you won't make it."
– Josh McDowell

"Without the Spirit of God, we can do nothing. We are ships without the wind, branches without sap, and coals without fire….we are useless."
– Charles Spurgeon

"A Bible that is falling apart usually belongs to someone who isn't."
– Charles Spurgeon

"Sin is the most expensive thing in the universe. If it is forgiven sin, it cost God his only son. If it is unforgiven sin, it costs the sinner his soul and an eternity in hell."
– Charles Finney

TIME WASTED

Never used, wasted time
Cannot be recovered

Time is the only
Measure of life

If ill spent or unplanned
There slips away life

Don't mark the sands of
Time with sloth

Never build yourself and
Children around the adage

A minute carefully spent
Can make the word a better place

No difference whether spent
At work or play

But counted out of life
With awareness, that….

A minute carefully spent
Can make the world a better place.

– John H. Knauf, Sr.

"The man with a cross no longer controls his destiny. He lost control when he picked up his cross. That cross immediately became to him a self-absorbing interest or overwhelming interference. No matter what he may desire to do there is but one thing he can do…..and that is move on toward the place of crucifixion.
– A.W. Tozer

Preach the gospel, and when necessary, use words.
– Usually attributed to St. Francis of Assisi

A great sales person once said "sometimes people need to be disturbed before they take action."
– Ben Feldman

All things (not just some things) work together for the good of them that love the Lord and are called according to His purpose. (whether we are on the mountain top or in the valley)
– Romans 8:28

"RELIGION COMPARED TO RELATIONSHIP"

The Lord is my shepherd, I
Lack nothing.
He makes me lie down in
Green pastures,
He leads me beside quiet waters.
He refreshes my soul.
He guides me along the right paths
For his namesake.
Even though I walk
Through the darkest valley
I will fear no evil,
For you are with me;
Your rod and your staff
They comfort me.
You prepare a table before me
In the presence of my enemies.
You anoint my head with oil;
My cup overflows.
Surely your goodness and love
Will follow me
All the days of my life,
And I will dwell in the house of
The Lord forever.
– Psalms 23

There is an account of a well-known man with great speaking abilities who gave an impressive recitation of Psalm 23. A member of his audience said he was more moved by the recitation of a lesser-known speaker. When asked why, he replied "Because he knows the Shepherd."

"Everyone has morals until it starts costing them something."
– John Knauf, Sr.

DO IT ANYWAY

People are often unreasonable and self-centered.
Forgive them anyway

If you are kind, people may accuse you of ulterior motives.
Be kind anyway

If you are honest, people may cheat you.
Be honest anyway

If you find happiness, people may be jealous.
Be happy anyway

The good you do today may be forgotten tomorrow.
Do good anyway

Give the world the best you have and it may never be enough.
Give your best anyway

For you see, in the end, it is between you and God.
It was never between you and them anyway.

– Mother Teresa

HUMOR ATTEMPS

A man called the church. The secretary answered. The man said "Is the hog at the trough?" She said if you're talking about our pastor you should have more respect. Then he said I have a thousand dollar donation. Then she said "OK, the big pig just walked in".

A hen went to a pig and proposed a breakfast for the farmer. The hen offered to provide the eggs and suggested the pig provide some ham. The pig responded: "that's just a contribution from you, but a total commitment from me."

The definition of an expert, is a stranger with a briefcase.

Have you noticed that everyone's financial planner is a genius?

Groucho Marks said I'll be a monkey's uncle. Excuse me while I go to the zoo to feed my nephew some peanuts.

Groucho Marks said I'd never want to be a part of a club that would have me as a member.

W.C.Fields alledgely was on his death bed reading a Bible. His friend said "I didn't know you were religious." and W.C. responded "I'm looking for a loop hole."

A FEW KEY PASSAGES FROM THE HOLY SCRIPTURES

"For God so loved the world, that He gave His only son, that whoever believes in Him should not perish but have eternal life." John 3:16

"For the wages of sin is death, but the free gift of God is eternal life through Christ Jesus our Lord." Romans 6:23

"Behold I stand at the door and knock. If anyone hears my voice and opens the door, I will come in." Revelation 3:20

We didn't earn Salvation, and we certainly don't deserve it, but it's a free gift available to everyone.

If you'd like to begin a personal relationship with Jesus today, please pray this prayer:

> Lord Jesus, I invite You into my life.
> I believe You died for me and that Your blood pays
> For my sin and provides me with the gift of eternal life.
> By faith I receive that gift, and
> I acknowledge You as my Lord and Savior. Amen.

> Happy trails to you until we meet again…

> John Knauf, Jr.
> Les Connell
> Darrell Badger

www.ingramcontent.com/pod-product-compliance
Lightning Source LLC
LaVergne TN
LVHW052007060526
838201LV00059B/3889